Everett D. Stark

Bimetallism and the Royal Commission

Everett D. Stark

Bimetallism and the Royal Commission

ISBN/EAN: 9783743334038

Manufactured in Europe, USA, Canada, Australia, Japa

Cover: Foto ©ninafisch / pixelio.de

Manufactured and distributed by brebook publishing software
(www.brebook.com)

Everett D. Stark

Bimetallism and the Royal Commission

Preface.

Her British Majesty in 1886 appointed a commission of twelve eminent financiers, to inquire into the causes of the recent changes in the ' 'relative values of Gold and Silver;'' with especial reference to the embarrassments thence accruing to the Indian Budget, but including also the wider commercial and industrial effects of those changes; and then to make such recommendations to Parliament as they deemed proper. They made their final report last October, making no recommendation as to remedial measures; but did report a mass of information more or less relevant to the question of causes; all of which properly digested makes a strong case against the experiment of occidental monometallism. Congress has ordered and made appropriation for the republication of that report in full, for the enlightenment of its own members upon the question of monetary legislation, now exigent.

Having given much study to the subject, I have been moved to analyze that Report and have commented upon it with some freedom. But with becoming modesty here, I submit my argument to the critical judgement of such of my countrymen as will take the pains to understand it.

E. D. STARK.

Cleveland, O., September 2, 1889.

BIMETALLISM

AND

THE ROYAL COMMISSION.

The Question Stated.

A PRECISE and clear Statement of a Problem goes far towards its solution. It would be hard to find a more grievous sin against the dialectical Canon implied in that proposition, than the putting of the question submitted by Her Majesty to this Commission.

To ask an investigation into the causes of the recent "changes in the relative values of gold and silver", is a most sorry and unpromising start-off. It befogs the whole question. Considering that Value is a Relation of two things, and not a property of

one alone, to talk about a change in the "relative
values", is to talk about a change of *relative relations*
of two things. That puts a strain upon the thinking
faculty. The whole matter is obfuscated in the outset. One would as soon tackle the changes in the
relativity of the Unrelated, or other metaphysical
abstruseness, as the causes of changes in the *relative*
market relation of two metals.

No doubt Her Majesty intended to call attention
to the changed market relation, or current swapping
rate of the two metals. Then why not say so?

If the impatient reader who fancies I convict
myself of hypercriticism by the confession that I
understand what is intended by the words, will go
with me a little deeper, to find the elementary fallacy
that is smuggled into the discussion by the words,
he will withdraw his imputation.

The words imply that each of the metals has
an independent and separate value, ascertainable and
statable in something the same way as we find the
comparative weight of two heavy bodies, *viz:*—by
placing each separately on the scales, observing the
weight-units registered, and then comparing the
numbers. Then, of course, the measuring unit would

be the Pound Sterling; though why it, rather than the more modest Rupee, should have that office in such an inquiry would be difficult to tell. Why it does have in this Royal Commission work, is the natural consequence of the fundamental error of method I shall try to expose.

In the nature of things there cannot be a Unit of Value, as there can be of Weight, Length, Time, Force, etc., any more than there can be a unit of Fit for a tailor. Like Fit, it is a relation,—a market relation. It is a relation of Market Equivalence. The value of a particular thing is *any other thing that swaps even for it* in the market. This is a definition, accurate, severe and exclusive as any in geometry. It will read backwards with the same cogency of affirmation as forwards,—and that is the test of a perfect definition.

We are accustomed to say of two things having a market equivalence, that they are of the same, or have the same value, which is true enough, but misleads, when understood to mean that they are so, in virtue of each having the same number of units of some subtile inherent quality called Value. The realistic bottom truth in such a case is expressed

by saying that these two things, by being brought
into that market relation, by the concurrence of two
minds, *are* (for that occasion) *each the value of the
other*, and the measuring or value-defining office. is
reciprocal and plenary. True, some inherent, desirable
quality in the things may be the ground of that
comparative estimation, but only when all culminates
in a market fact, actual or supposititious, is value
affirmable. In virtue of such an act or fact only,
can the notion of value emerge in thought at all.

If the student of the subject would attain to clear
and competent thinking, let him employ the critical
device of substituting in the propositions of popular
discussion, in the place of the word value, its definition. He will be amazed at the amount of fatuity
disclosed in current discourse. Or if he does not
like *Market Equivalence*, let him try a definition of
his own devising; but by all means adopt some one,
and try it, for the method will work him out to
clear and sound results.

Just here, I would most earnestly entreat my self-
complacent single-standard reader to disabuse himself
of the erroneous notion that this paper is simply a
bother over the proprieties of expression, born of a dis-

position for verbal and dialectical niceties. If the words and propositions do not truthfully stand for actual facts, forces, and conditions of our daily business transactions, and are not apposite to the economic situation and corrective of grave, practical errors, then indeed are they but idle babble. But they are not that; they are far from merely verbal criticism. They constitute the germinal conceptions of any and all competent thinking on the subject.

But lest my unindulgent reader will not have the patience voluntarily to subject his own thinking, or his own favorite doctrines to the critical test I have recommended, let me do it by application to the statement reported to have been made by Lord Salisbury, on his feet in Parliament. He said:

" The great fall in prices in recent years is not due to any change in the value of gold."

Now make the substitution:

" The great fall in the rate at which goods swap for (gold) money (prices) is not due to any change in the rate at which gold (money) swaps for goods ! ! "

So long as such utterances pass before the assembled wisdom of England, without being drowned by derisive cheers and cat-calls; so long as the great

British heart is calmed by such a proposition into complacency at the present abnormal swapping relation between money and goods, it is high time for somebody to come forward and puncture its oracular emptiness. It is a piece of magnificent bathos.

The pestilent fallacy lurking in the words criticised, takes on robust proportions and dictatorial airs. in Her Majesty's specifications as to,

.   "Whether, the said changes are due,
(1.) To the depreciation of Silver ; or
(2.) To the appreciation of Gold ; or
(3.) To both these causes."

and dooms the whole quest, so far as a rational treatment of its vast array of facts is concerned, to emptiness and vanity.

See the absurdity to which such a putting commits the inquisitors; and from which none of them except one, (Mr. Barbour), were able to extricate themselves. They proceed to stultify themselves by the astounding proposition, that while it is certain that prices, at a gold valuation all over the world, of commodities generally, have fallen at least 30%, there is yet no evidence that it was "due to" the appreciation in the value of gold ; nor, indeed, was there any evidence of any appreciation of gold at all!!

The inquiry as put, is as though it were asked whether the change in the condition of a newly married pair was *due* to his marrying her, or her marrying him, "or to both these causes." Whether the depression of trade is *due to* there being fewer sales, *or* to fewer purchases, or to both; whether this change in the market relation of the two metals was *due to* the fact that, whereas an ounce of gold used to swap for $15\frac{1}{2}$ oz. of silver, it now swaps for 25 oz., OR to the fact that, while an ounce of silver used to buy $\frac{2}{31}$ oz. of gold, it now buys only $\frac{1}{25}$:—OR to both. In fine, whether a situation or market fact stated in one form was "due to" the same fact stated in another form of words.

The equality of the sides of a triangle is not the cause of the equality of its angles nor the converse. We may, indeed, say by way of logical demonstration that the sides are equal *because* the angles are, or the angles are equal *because* the sides are, but our "because" is not a cause, for it expresses a static, not a causal relation. Appreciation of one term of a swap is the same fact as depreciation of the other. These are not two separable facts, but are sempiternally fixed and interdependent relations that can never be separated in thought. It is nonsense raised to a power, to talk of a changed

swapping rate of two things being *caused* by the
appreciation of the swapping rate of one *or* the depreciation of the rate of the other, and then set out
solemnly in search of which it is. Those two things
appreciation and depreciation are correlatives and co-
existants and can never exist apart.

At the risk of offending the proprieties of public
discussion, and all the while protesting my high respect
for the members of this Commission, for their great intelligence and distinguished service in other fields, I
nevertheless make bold to affirm, that any one who,
admitting a fall of general prices 30% at a gold valuation, yet says there is no evidence that gold has appreciated in value; or who does not see that in so admitting he affirms a 43% appreciation of gold, betrays an
intellectual incompetence for the discussion. Nor does
the fact that the vast majority of financiers are in that
case, daunt me. Though I am fain to crave pardon
for a pedagogical and assertative tone, the elementary
character of the principle brought in question, the
deep and wide spread error in regard to it, the
scornful pretentiousness of that error, and the gravity
of the practical issues involved are my warrant for
such a device of polemic emphasis. I must therefore

repeat, even to weariness, that the value of a money unit is what it will swap for, and it is simply going round in a vicious circle, to define such a unit or its value, in money terms. Computation of the value of silver in terms of Rupees would lead to the same conclusion of absolute stability of silver, which the Commission came to in regard to gold, by computing in terms of English money. It is an unpardonable imbecility in such a quest not to be able to get out of the conventional groove of a mere accountant. This defect is so wide spread and inveterate, that I well appreciate the risk I run by this bold characterization of it. Something more than mere opinion must be my warrant, if I am to be saved from the just scorn of noble minds, for such seeming temerity. I am content to abide the verdict, so I get a patient hearing.

The critical question in a discussion of value or value-change is: Value *in what?* and if the *what* is the same thing, though under another name, as the thing you are valuing, you will be defining a notation merely, or saying a thing is equal to the sum of the parts into which you have divided it. There is absolutely nothing else by reference to which we can

value a unit of money, except commodities, and when
we say goods, in general have fallen 30% as to pounds
sterling, then to every competent intelligence the same
breath affirms a 43% appreciation of the pound.

Man is an appraising animal. Appraisment is
the crowning moment of his business activity. He
may survey his acres, count his herds and bushels,
weigh, number and inventory; but it is all naught, till
appraisment is made. When all is translated into a
money equivalent, verifiable by the current market
rating, he knows for the first time whether his enterprise is a success or a failure, and to what extent. To
this test must all business submit. To "make money"
is its chief motive. But if the unit of valuation has
itself *an* depreciated, as shown by a fall in the general
range of prices, then the appraisment cheats the enterprise by so much, and will turn what might have
been a moderate profit into a loss. Not that a Constant Valuator could save unskillfulness and unthrift
from failure, or guaranty stability of price in every
particular product. It is normal and beneficent that
goods should go up and down in price. Rise and fall
constitute the automatism of re-directing and re-
distributing the productive energy. But with a

valuator constant by reference to the aggregate of products, there will always be an inviting rise in some allied industry for every particular fall. What under a false valuator is a general paralysis, becomes under a true one, merely a healthy process of re-adjustment.

It should be noted that a great and permanent fall in some particular thing may not be an evil at all. The occupations related to steel, petroleum, passenger fares and freight rates generally have prospered contemporaneously with a fall of $\frac{1}{5}$, $\frac{9}{10}$ and $\frac{19}{20}$ respectively. But this is because there has been a much higher ratio of increase in their consumption. Something of benefit will accrue to money by reason of discoveries and inventions. So our demand of stability by reference to the great staples is a moderate one.

Increased productivity and the abundance it brings, is industrial progress and marks an advancing Civilization. It ought to increase proportionally the assessable value of the common wealth. That industrial progress and abundance, from being an unqualified beneficence, as in the order of nature it would be, is by an inequitable valuator turned into a calamity. It gives us so called "plethora of goods" and hard times. To find an equitable, stable valuator we must go below the temporary and local fashion—must root deep into the subsoil of universal human nature in the valuing habit, and have regard to the automatic quantity relations of the material of money to other productions. No one man or set of men is competent to say how much money there ought to be, or when its increase ought to stop. It is the arrogance of a usurped prerogative for any official to put a limit upon the quantity of primary money. That is the same vice only infinitely more mischievous, because more subtle, as the limitation on coal or wall paper, etc., and has the same sinister animus, though more or less unconsciously so, for it is natural for us to think that which is advantageous to our special vocations is also promotive of the general good. The spontaneous output of the mines is the natural and salutary regulator of the money volume, and so of its value. I do not refer to secondary or representative money. Another law obtains there. Of intrinsic money, overflowing abundance—all that human skill and energy will produce—is beneficent, and in the line of the general well being, the same in kind, only in higher degree, as is abundance of every other product of human endeavor.

The spirit of the Act of 1878 has from the first been violated by the Treasury administration. Its policy has been to treat standard silver coin simply as a subsidiary coinage carried up to a fiat value by limitation. and to affect great solicitude as to getting it in circulation. We do not want it as a subsidiary coinage serving as small change, kept to an artificial gold value by limitation. We want no "value created by legislation", in the obnoxious sense imputed to us by the one-metallists. That. in its most injurious form is now effected by the policy of the mint.

The word Value in the constitution, conferring the power to coin money and "regulate the value thereof" means Algebraic value merely and not commercial. It was never intended that Congress should use its power to foist upon standard coin by legislation, a commercial value beyond what belongs naturally to it. We insist upon rock bottom in the value of money, that our unit of valuation shall not under the specious pretext of "improving the Standard" be put upon the swollen and artificial basis of a single metal, but shall be restored to the level to which gold itself will return when compelled to share equally with silver the privileges of the mint.

There are three distinct offices or modes of use of money.

The First and least evolved is where it is a word serving merely to mark a scale of relative estimation of things bartered. Nothing passes, not even a symbol and the word is empty of meaning. "Macoot" is as good as "Dollar" in that capacity.

The Second, is where money serves purely as a medium of exchange for goods: the exchange not being regarded as completed till the tokens are again passed off for other goods; In this function, anything, a ticket, a paper promise, will do so long as it goes. Where transactions are quickly closed and have little relation to the past or future, a piece of paper, even though counterfeit, may do the work.

The Third is where money is itself, at bottom, a commodity—a tangible, deliverable product, for which other property may be exchanged, for the the purpose of being permanently stored. In virtue of this office, it becomes a mode of investment wherein its understood relations to the past and future are emphasized and it becomes a standard of deferred payment.

In this office its efficiency and equity depend

upon its *stability and constancy of value.* The first
and second modes of its use may be cast out of the
reckoning in this discussion, for in those lower offices,
tho' important, a money fitted for the third will be
perfectly adapted. In this Third office it is, that
a money may be beneficent in its operation, or may
become an instrument of unmeasured wrong and
disaster; all the more deadly because disguised. In
this Third office, I repeat, constancy of value, linking
the past, the present, and the future in one equitable
solidarity is the paramount concern. That great
word "Dollar" and the thing it stands for, in taking
upon itself the duty of valuing all things, should
itself stand true and steadfast to that high trust. It
should not be seduced from efficiency in that, its chief
beneficence, by appreciation. As a form of investment, a mode of storing earnings, the interest it yields
when loaned, is its only legitimate profit or income.
It has no business to increase in value, as a piece
of real estate or other property may properly do;
for its fitness as a valuator and Standard of deferred
payment is thereby impaired. With that impair-
ment, follows inefficiency in its chief use. It will not
function, will not transact. It accumulates in the

centres of trade and grows obese. refusing to take a hand in business. Hoarding. appreciation, low interest, low profits, want of confidence, hard times, are all concomitant phenomena, are phases of a single economic condition, are the common effects of contraction. So are depreciation, large profits, high interest rates, business activity and prosperity, money all out eager to buy, good times—concurrent phenomena and the necessary result of expansion of the money volume.

Increase of the number of depositors in savings banks is commonly pointed to as a proof of improved conditions. I say no. So far as they indicate thrift. the habit of saving and the ability to save, of course it is well. But considering the mode of it, it tells the same sad story of the necessary unproductiveness of capital. To my view. an increasing number of small house-owners, homes well equipped with the appliances of education and culture for the children, and an assurance of steady employment, would tell a better story as an indication of an increasing wealth and the activity of wealth-creating forces. That "the times" are such as to compel a hoarding in savings banks at a low interest on peril of "losing money" is the evil we complain of.

In England, the exigencies of the Indian Budget, and in money centres generally, the conveniences of foreign exchange, (conventionalized to mean simply money changing) have domineered the whole question of Bimetallism. That dominance is as illegitimate from that side, as is the distress cry of the "silver interest" from our own camp. These are but partial phases of the great subject, important indeed to the interest immediately implicated, but contemptible when thrust into the fore-front of a question involving all the high moral and industrial interests of society. The "price of silver" is a petty matter, and the difficulties of collecting a few hundred millions sterling by creditor and administrative England, out of a fixed Rupee income, make a great outcry, but is of no consequence to anybody in this country, and to few of the common people in Europe. Whether "exchange" is kept within 1% of variation by a fixed par of $4.86, or runs up to $5, $6 or $10 to the Pound seems to moneymongers of commanding importance. They no doubt really believe that such unstable relation would imply some fiction, falsity, and insecurity in our money. But the high interests of society are more implicated with the equity of time contracts, with the just distribution of our rapidly increasing wealth among the agencies creative of it, and with the general industrial health and content. It is a thousand times more important that 'there should be an approximately constant "par of exchange" between our money on the one hand and goods on the other, than that $4.86 should be a Pound.

There is no occasion to change our legal rating to conform to the present constrained and artificial ratio. After both metals shall have been freely coined for a, few years we shall know more about their normal relation. There is no occasion to consider the expediency of lessening the weight of our gold coins at present to conform to the European $15\frac{1}{2}$. When there is a demand for inter-national action it will be time enough for that.

The movement rife in the sixties, toward inter-national symmetry and unity in weights and measures and a decimal notation, out of which this one-metal-lism sprung, was rational, and aimed at a desirable end. But its reasons and theories were wide of the mark in relation to money. A metre, litre, gramme, etc., will not shrink and swell by the varying estimation and urgency of need in the user. They are fixed units in their respective categories—fixed, I mean, and un-

varying in the measuring office. But the quantum of
value that a money unit, being a unit of a money metal,
will take on, depends upon a thousand and one
changes in the varying situation of the user. Every
time a transaction is made involving the measuring
office of money, so much metal must be delivered
over for the goods—the voluntary parting with and
delivery of it constituting the measuring process. If
delivery is by symbol or representative devices then
still must the metal be there, ready to verify the
symbol, or it is convicted of fraud. So while a single
yard stick will measure with uniformity, (whatever
may be the scramble for it for use,) or may upon the
instant be indefinitely multiplied, a single dollar
would be a wild valuator. The number of money
units obtainable is a controlling factor in determining
the quantum of value a unit measures, and constancy
as a valuator over-rides every other consideration. It
sinks international symmetry, or even sameness of
material into insignificance.

These words, Constancy, Stability, Uniformity
and Proximate Fixity, in the value of money, are the
same economic fact as stability of prices; for if money
maintains a constant swapping rate to goods, it goes

without saying that goods are constant to it. Price is a ratio of two terms, and when a ratio changes, it changes with relation to both terms alike, only in the opposite direction. Men who will quite agree, (because it is a commonplace of economic doctrine) that stability in the value of money is of chief moment in its behavior, are often all at sea when called upon to tell just what that means, other than fixity of weight in standard coins, and will stare at you when you tell them that our money as at present constituted, stands impeached in that regard, by the fact of a long-continued period of low prices. It is low prices, and the probability of still lower prices that gives importance to this whole question. It is the difference between Hard Times and Good Times. And whether or not people can understand the nature of value and the law of value-change, they do know and appreciate that difference. Guarantee a period of improving prices on up toward those of 1873, and a reasonable probability of stability after that, and not a willing hand will be idle, nor a pretext for privation in all the land.

Unlimited coinage is the one measure competent to that end. Coinage up to the maximum now allowed

by law will be a long step in that direction. It is
against the general good to improve prices of some
particular product by arbitrary restriction of out-put,
and it would be calamitous to raise them by a general
restriction, if, indeed, such a thing were practicable, as
it is not. We want good prices in the midst of an
abundant harvest and busy mills and shops. That can
come only by an abundance of money. It is the money
factor in the ratio of money to goods, over which
government assumes control. A pretty muddle
they have made of it too, by cutting loose from the
steadying effect of silver which is so firmly fixed in the
valuing office, that its occidental outlawry has not
phased its steadfastness. It still stands true in the prime
and paramount office of good money, viz: in stable
market relation to products. An ounce of it will buy
as much as it would in 1873 or any time in the past
century. Its changed relation to gold must continue
to be stigmatized as a " Fall of Silver " to serve the
purpose of the monometallic imposture. A truer
diagnosis of the situation for Statemanship in monetary
legislation would be the " Rise of Gold,"
for surely in such a contention goods is the rightful
umpire. But Mono-metallism could not stand except

by abuse of language and obscuration of economic law at the arrogant dictation of the "Pun' Sterling."

There is no grounds of hope for help in this business from England. The key to the English view is found on Page 90, Part II.—Final Report.— Sec. 128, of the Royal Commission. That section reads as follows :

" It must be remembered too, that this country is largely a creditor country of debts payable in gold, and any change which entails a rise in the price of commodities generally ; that is to say, a diminution of the purchasing power of gold would be to our disadvantage."

When Creditor England takes precedence of Industrial England in the solicitude of her statesman, the end is not far off. Note carefully that the solicitude expressed does not involve any possible repudiation or failure of exact and full discharge of contract obligations. Not that—it has reference simply to a policy which will increase the Commodity Equivalence of the Pound, as against one that will check that increase and probably turn it into a decrease. These men do not see how that vaulting selfishness is one

　　　*　　*　　*　　which o'erleaps its sad'l

　　And falls on the other side——

There are financiers and—financiers. Surviving from ruder conditions, there is a greed that accounts other people's misfortunes and times of general distress as most opportune for shrewd money makers. So they are, in a way. But there is a better way. A financiering that inaugurates great beneficences and amasses a fortune by fostering wealth-producing agencies and helps everybody, is pleasanter to contemplate than one which occupies itself in manufacturing "corners," limiting production, and that can't feel quite sure it has advantaged itself, unless it can see clearly that somebody else has lost. The instinct of England's business men is sounder and more alert. It will carry her active investable capital elsewhere, and she will 'be left with her pride, respectabilities, traditions and titles—which are indeed no small outfit, and will no doubt stand her in good stead for many generations to come. But God pity her wage earners, unless the overflow of beneficence of our better monetary policy shall bring them relief.

The Pound by statutory definition now these three-quarters of a century, has been a gold coin only, and any change of definition will be sure to meet the charge of legislative immorality. It is wicked, you know, to change a fixed money definition,—*i. e.* it is wicked, if it has the economic effect to lessen its value! But the financial conscience was not hurt by the Act of 1816, nor by Germany's change, plump from one metal to the other. Wall Street was not shocked by the attempted,—but thank God, not quite accomplished, change of definition in 1873 from the 412½ *gr.* unit. Therefore with us the coast is quite clear. We need make no change in definition, no assault on the dictionary or the decimal notation for whatever a Dollar is, it must be 100 cents.

Will not some one from the gold camp tell us what will be the effect upon prices if we have unlimited coinage? 'Of course the silver dollar will then have the same value as, will be interchangeable with, 412½ *grs.* silver. But what effect will it have upon the price of iron. cotton, meat, *etc.*? Will some intelligent silver-phobiist enlighten us on that all important subject? Please do not regale us with that quintessent assininity of the ante-inaugural letter of our late President, predicting that this continued coinage of silver would drive gold to a premium and so out of circulation, make money scarce, cause panic prices, and yet our money would be too cheap by 25%!! The notion of prices being lowered panicward by a threatened inundation of cheap legal-tender money is a novelty in economic doctrine deserving a patent. Still, if we may assume their sincerity, that doctrine was level with the Wall street intelligence. No, not those utter incompatabilities prophesied by Mr. Cleveland, but some plausible reason why free coinage would not restore the prices of 1873. Any one who should affirm that it would not go far in that direction, would prove himself wanting in economic intelligence.

The assumption that units of gold, labeled with a money name and so made a "standard of value", (whatever that may mean), becomes thereby no longer amenable to the law of value-change is a most mischievous error. There is but one law of value-change, and that binds every economic quantity alike. The value of a thing, described by whatever name, is the estimate put on it by trading men, as expressed by and in the other term in the trade, and relative scarcity ·and plenty of money has the same effect on *it*, as it does on every other transferable object of desire. To a properly equipped intelligence, the simple fact that for a succession of years, alike in seasons of plenteous and lean harvests, the great staples have ruled low in price proves a scarcity of money. When it takes five pecks of wheat to buy a dollar, then, surely is there a scarcity of dollars in relation to wheat; and if the same depression obtains in goods generally, then is there a general scarcity of money proven. Credit and other familiar devices may cushion the impact of a local or temporary scarcity, but once it becomes general and protracted the law will not be balked of its effect.

By the fall in prices the taxable value of all property is lessened; energy, skill and activity in production is discouraged, and who is benefited by it? Nobody: —unless the selfish reflection of the monied man that he is not so badly off as the enterpriser, is a benefit. True, his money units will each stand for more goods and he may fancy himself richer, but he cannot harvest his gains if prices still rule low and lower. Every industry and useful occupation suffers. The income from loanable funds is cut down with the decay of profits of business. Our Savings Banks pay 4 *per cent*. With improved prices and business

activity it would resume its old time rate of 6 per
cent. Take out 2½ *per cent.* fixed charges for taxes
(honestly assessed) and the net income would be
doubled.

One man is cheerful and an optimist under
falling prices. He is not many in the census enumer-
ation and does not count for much in the world's
work, though his name is, not unfrequently, conspicuous
on subscriptions for charity. But he is high toned.
and that makes him weighty and numerous. He is
the man of fixed money income. fixed by reference
to, and at a time of high prices or cheap money.
He is content it should so remain and he be re-
lieved from any reinvestment. With him high
commercial honor. high standard of money and increasing value of money, are synonomous terms. The
centers of capital adopt his high tone and his ethics.
It gets into the lobbies and dominates monetary
legislation. and is " played " upon an honest people.
because the man himself more than half believes
his to be the true view. The Professor adopts it
by instinct for he is a man of a fixed salary. Then
the "Able Editor" elaborates it by sarcasm at the poor
crank who would "make business lively and everybody

rich by flooding the country with cheap money." But seriously why should not money be cheap, as cheap as 412½ *grs.* of silver, say, or three pecks of wheat instead of five. Not a producer nor a man in any vocation closely related to production, but would say it were a consummation devoutedly to be wished could there be a rise in prices all along the line, without any natural or artificial diminution of production. But there is a vague feeling, born in part of a sad paper inflation experience, that makes them distrust "cheap money" as having some how concealed in it a fiction or deception, which will surely have its day of reckoning and retribution. Such feelings come up from the depths of our moral consciousness and are worthy of all respect. It is, however, a mistaken one in this application. Silver money is a world's money—international money—which will always go at its commodity or bullion value to pay international balances and go to stay, from the country which has more than its proportion. It is a commodity money, not a promise or token money amenable to governmental caprice as to its volume. The cheapness is in no sense a lessening of the weight or intrinsic quality of our long established legal standard and definition. The word "cheap" often has a flavor of disparagement as to intrinsic excellence. All of that implication should be taken out of the word, when, as here, it refers purely to what accrues to the thing by reason of its plentifulness.

Let any one who fears some wide departure in the market relation of silver money to goods, reflect a moment upon the spontaneous character of the forces determinant of its quantity-relation to products generally. The economic man seeks the occupation that is most remunerative to himself. When, many centuries hence, if ever, the "Silver Sink" of the Orient is full, and when it is still so plenty here as that $412\frac{1}{2}$ *grs.* of it will buy only 20 lbs. of wheat or less, *i. e.* wheat $3 and upward, then will there be but little temptation for the boys to leave the farm for the mines. Automatic adjustment constitutes the economic harmonies which are at one with the divine order every where. It is at the bottom of the entire theory of a Commodity money. If under any pretext, that automatism is to be repudiated, then by all odds it were better to adopt an intelligently regulated fiat money system.

No doubt there will be a great increase of production of both metals in the near future. All the indications point that way; but careful students believe the increasing demand for money in the rapid opening to civilization of great populations will take it all in, at a value fully up to that of 1873.

If by free coinage, money is cheapened 30 % then the assessable value of property will be raised correspondingly, will it not? If the effect stops there who is hurt by it? Is it not plain that such a change would be accordant with the everlasting equities, if that excess of value accrued to "*Dollar*" in consequence of the surreptitious Act. of 1873. But everybody knows it would not stop there in its economic effect. It would put every wealth-creating energy to its utmost tension, and so would increase the quantity of assessable things as well as put a higher appraisment on those we have. This will be quite different from a "merely nominal" increase of wealth. Though why a valuation by a unit of silver, standing true as it does, and constant as it was in 1873 as a valuator, should be any more "merely nominal" than an appraisment by gold, it would be difficult to tell. I would respectfully ask this eloquent declaimer against

legislation tending to decrease the value of money—
How about legislation to increase it, and the destruc-
tion by act of Congress of a part of the assessable
value of all existing property in 1873? And the
industrial stagnation that followed—has that any
ethical character? Civilization has paid dearly for
the imposture of a "High Standard," at the arrogant
dictation of the "British Pun.'"

All this argument is no disparagment of gold as
a money metal. Our claim is, we want a legal constitution of money that builds upon the automatic
adjustment of an immemorial past, and gives guaranty
of normal relation to goods for generations to come.
That adjustment has always proceeded on a valuator
constituted on silver with gold as a subordinate ally—
an invaluable aid. We want the guaranty of stability,
which long ages of uses with great nations will give.
not one that depends upon the manipulatory devices
of great financiers. We want a money constitution
that will vindicate its excellence by uniformity of value
over long periods of time, as gold, even in conjunction
with silver, has not. Not that an absolute level through
the centuries is possible, but one that binds the past,
present, and future to an approximate constancy of

prices. This is the demand of science, of conscience and of statesmanship, lifted out of the clash of contending interests and the bias of classes. This is "Good Money," a just "Measure." This is honest equivalence. It is an altogether secondary matter how gold and silver may rate in the market to each other. No doubt the one under our legal rating, that shall have the least purchasing power in the world's market will be the practical Dollar, the Dollar ·of account; as it will certainly be the most equitable, and its free use will surely bring the other down towards the ratio of 1:16. Our wheat and other exports will exchange in Europe for as much silk, cutlery or what-not under a silver valuation as under a gold one. A prudent man will not dogmatize as to quantities where the factors are so involved and multifarious as here, but he may assert the direction of tendency. Still I share with many competent students, the opinion that unlimited coinage here will restore the ratio of 16. But taking the extremest view of the monometallic alarmist *viz.*: a continued ratio of 1:20 or 25, it is plain that the business of the country will be on a more solid basis on silver than on gold. The Royal Commission has abundantly shown this. (See Barbour's Note 22).

They affirm what was well known before and all the testimony concurred in the opinion that Indian prices are normal to the past. If a premium on Gold accrues, then will European prices be so much lower than ours. And so, without the intervention of custom houses, we shall be upon a higher range of prices, with this additional advantage, that it will be uniform in its operation on all products. That will be a better mode of raising prices than strikes, lock-outs, and combines to limit production. Such experiments are but the blind and ineffectual attempts to redress an oppressive situation not understood.

The Commission have deemed it important to find how much of the "change is due to causes affecting Silver alone," how much to "causes affecting Gold alone" and the same of goods. Of course they find great improvements in the arts and appliances of production, but fail to see how that fact tends necessarily to appreciate the value of money *i. e.* increase its purchasing power. (Do not forget that the value of money *is* its purchasing power.) They are charged also to find how much of the (found or assumed) depreciation of silver is "due to increase of supply and how much to diminution of demand," and the same as to the appreciation of gold, if they find any appreciation. Such a quest leads nowhere by their methods. It has no bottom, begins and ends in the boundless void. The same fundamental vice runs through the entire report, viz.: a failure to apprehend the purely relational character of supply, of demand, and their necessary joint and co-operant action in every value-change. This failure is but a phase of their elementary error in economic statics, i. e. the Nature of Value.

Let me illustrate the futility of any attempt at studying the several moments of value-change apart from their constituting relations. A. has a dollar, but would have a bushel of wheat. B. has a bushel of wheat, but prefers a dollar. Their desires come to fruition in a trade. Now a trade is the central subject matter of economic science. Trade furnishes the material for its analyses and theories. Without trade there can be no value-phenomena at all. In the case supposed, science says that the dollar (carrying of course, with it, by implication, the subjective or desire element) constitutes the money supply and the wheat demand. The bushel is the wheat supply and the money demand, each term in the trade is, therefore, reciprocally a supply and a demand in relation

to the other term, in the same sense as every
ordinary mercantile transaction is both a sale and a
purchase according as it is regarded from one side or
the other, and is yet one insoluble transaction. Only
a little reflection on the interdependent and reciprocal
character of these forces will be required in order
to show the impossibility of confining a study of this
sort to "causes affecting gold alone" and causes
affecting wheat alone—for the effect we are in search
of, is effect upon value, and value is always extrinsic,
being the other term in the trade.

A sociologist would make but little headway in
his study of the psychology of marriage, by confining his attention to the "causes affecting the lad
alone" and to "causes affecting the lass alone", for
they are each to the other the essential and operative cause, marriageward.

Considered as a question between the two metals
alone, and out of relation to all other economic quantities, *i. e.* considering the change in their market relation simply, a competent intelligence would say at
once, that if a former market equivalence of $15\frac{1}{2}$:1 had
now become one of 31:1, the extraction of moonshine
from cucumbers would be a respectable and renum-

erative industry as compared to a solemn endeavor to find whether it was a depreciation of one or an appreciation of the other, and in what proportion to distribute it, if it is both. Then having solemnly settled that question of statics, to launch into the realm of Causes on that line, to set out to properly distribute the portion "due to each," would be like locating the aforesaid moonshine industry in the fourth dimension of space. Any schoolboy ought to tell them that the change supposed *is* a doubled value of one *and* a halved value of the other; and the question as to the causes of such a change must have in it, and following the "due to"— more apt words than depreciation and appreciation—if the inquirer would be saved from the charge of imbecility. To make any valuable progress in that general search we must have some third economic quantity to serve as a "standard" for that special occasion. It was hardly to be expected that Her Majesty would take any other than a purely insular view of it, and consequently the British Pound, which is simply a unit of gold, became the standard for the Commission.

Well, what should have been the umpire in determing which of the two metals had been misbehaving to cause the change? Why, clearly, some other product.

Or, considering that they are both money metals and in that—their chief use—they stand over against *all* other purchasable things—unless some one fairly representative product can be found, then a composite commodity unit must be got. Such units are the basis of the so-called " Index numbers " of market statisticians, and they are many and variously constituted; any of them are sufficiently accurate for the general purpose. So far as my own reading goes, I do not hesitate to give precedence to that devised by W. M. Grosvenor, diagramatized in the Congressional Record for April 15, 1886. The use of such an index number or composite commodity unit is to get the changes in the market relation of money to goods, not to each one in particular, but to them in the aggregate. They all tell substantially the same story, viz.: a fall of about 30% of aggregate prices, *i. e.* an appreciation of about 43% of gold money, whereas the market relation of goods to silver has not materially changed. Wherefore the finding of the Commission but for the Blind, Bullish, Bigotry of the British Pound would have been that monometallic money is responsible for the " fall of silver " and the low prices.

The amount of labor required to produce a unit

of commodities, at some previous period, as compared to what the same labor will produce now is a vicious criterion of amount of value-change in money or anything else; because a stupid, slavish, unskilled labor unit, unaided by machinery, has no definable quantity-comparison for any purpose of Economics, with a labor unit of an intelligent, free, skilled operative, equipped with modern economizing appliances. Any serviceable comparison must be between the now and the then of the same thing. Not a unit of skill, of strain, of privation, endurance or of service,— if such units could be defined in respect of, or on the basis of time, intensity or dignity,–but a unit of definite products whose quality has undergone no material change, must constitute the subject matter of such a comparison. The Metals, Lumber, Meat, the Cereals, Fabric-Staples, *etc.*, are alone competent to speak here.

The investigation into the Causes of Value-change is a fool's errand, where the student is ignorant of Economic Statics and elementary definitions. If he supposes that changes in a something (value) which is essentially a Ratio, can be profitably studied as to the causes of it by confining the attention to one factor

alone, and proceeds upon the incompetent assumption
that the ratio of one factor may go kiting all the way
from the nadir to the zenith, while the ratio of the
other factor remains unmoved, he will very likely
come to the same conclusion as the Commission has,
at § 99 Part II.

" We may summarize our conclusions upon this part of the case
as follows : We think that the fall in prices of commodities may be
in part due to au appreciation of gold, but to what extent this has
affected prices we think it impossible to determine with any approach
to accuracy.

" May be in part due! " " Impossible to determine" indeed ! Well, we should think so ! Upon the
question as to whether the upright distance between the
eaves and sidewalk is *due to* the sidewalk being so much
below the eaves, or the eaves so much above the
sidewalk, we think "it may be in part due to the "
eaves being above the sidewalk, but to what extent,
etc--It puts a great strain upon one's courtesy to
refrain from characterizing such twaddle as it deserves.

A very pertinent line of inquiry would have been
this:--having found a great increase in the quantity of
goods, which is one (objective) factor of the rate which
price is, to see whether the causes of that increase were
of a transient or permanent character and were likely to

continue. Having found as they must the affirmative of that point, to-wit, that the goods-factor both on its objective, or quantity, side and on its subjective, or need-and-desire side, are permanently increasing, the increase had come to stay, as constant conditions, over which government had no control, there would be nothing more to be said about them and they could give their undivided attention to the money factor. As to that factor, they must quickly have found that the need and desire for money was increasing, but that upon a single metal, money had fallen out of normal and beneficent relation to goods generally as well as to silver. Its swapping rate with goods has been enhanced about 43 % and as the lessening of goods could not be thought of as either desirable or practicable, only one thing remained, that was to increase the money volume. But so trammelled up were they with the preconception that the Pound is an infallible guide, or that if it erred, it would be all on the creditor's side, that they could not find anything to do or recommend to relieve the situation.

Admitting as I gladly, nay, proudly, do, all that can be claimed for lessened cost of production, I still insist that that is no justification of the increase

of the purchasing power of money. Not one
jot of that increase belongs to "*Dollar*." Enough, if it
will buy as much of useful things as it did before
these inventions. All the increased efficiency they
have given belongs, not to money, but to the labor and
enterprise giving the increase. A money that absorbs
into its maw, if not all, then a large part of that increase is the guilty cause of the inequitable distribution of our rapidly increasing wealth.

The industrial strain is not properly a contest
between the rich and the poor, the debtor and creditor,
the laborer and the capitalist, or either of them and
the enterpriser, nor employer and employee. It only
seems so, and may take that form just as a diseased
condition of the body will break out at an old hurt or
accidental scratch or strain. It is a contest between
one form of investment and another form: rather
it is a mal-adjustment, a dislocation of proper relation
of money to goods. It is a difficulty caused by the
legal impartation to money, of something that dis-
qualifies it for its supreme function of valuator, and
makes it the most advantageous mode of investment,
imparting to it the power of increase different from
the legitimate one of interest-drawing; so that it

seems to increase in idleness at the expense of every other form of property. Not the enhanced burden of debt, public and private,—though that is fair ground of complaint, but not that chiefly. It is because an appreciating money is a plethoric, a sluggish money, refusing to function in the beneficent use of equitable transfer and re-transfer of goods, but instead accummulating in the centers of trade, condemned to a low interest, because to buy is to "lose money." This appreciation is not in fact a positive gain to the moneyed man himself, for he is only saving himself from loss, if there is to be no turning point, so he can realize his seeming gains by buying. The legal constitution of money is responsible, not he who does the best he can to save himself from loss.

Bonds drawing only 4%, commanding 25% premium, tells the same melancholy tale of the unprofitableness of capital in productive enterprises. In a rapidly expanding country like ours, under healthy monetary conditions 8% would not be a high interest. Under such conditions holders would gladly surrender their bonds at their face value.

By this time it will have become apparent to the attentive reader that, as stated in the outset, a misapprehension of the nature of value, perpetuated by crude and unclear language bars the way to the solution. Failure there makes all discussion of the causes of value-change profitless. This incompetence will be more apparent by the character of the current objections to free coinage.

A foremost and much-speaking publicist has gone to great pains to show that cotton, tea, wheat, etc., are produced and marketed more cheaply than formerly and that that is the reason why prices have fallen, and therefore appreciation of money is not the *cause* of it. No intelligent person could perpetrate the folly of claiming that appreciation has *caused* it. All any one from this side ever pretended is that from your own showing money *has* greatly appreciated, and by reason of that fact, the experiment of mono-metallism has proved a dismal failure. We claim also that the guilty *cause* of this great fall of prices is, in a perfectly proper and legitimate sense of the word, *cause*, as giving the conditions that made it possible—the Act of 1873. But for that Act our money could not have broken loose from silver. If your tailor assures you that your discomfort is not caused by any change in the fit of your coat, but is owing to the fit of your body having changed, and should launch into an anatomical and dietary disquisition to prove it, all as a justification of his refusal to make any change in the coat, he would parallel the wisdom of this publicist. But with your tailor you would probably with some impatience and sarcasm, tell him he had better extract the "fit" out of the coat, and lay it away as a fixed unit of fit measurement, and test all coats by it in respect to their fitness, and giving him further "particular fits" for his crotchety fittiness, go to some other tailor who had notions adapted to the situation, and get such changes made in your coat as would make it suitable for its office.

Another suggests that if appreciation of money (we must help him out, for maybe he means insufficiency of money) had caused the fall of prices, then would there be an exactly parallel fall in all commodities alike; whereas a few special products have actually risen in price:—as though there must of necessity be an unchanging market relation among the different products under an appreciating, any more than a non-appreciating money. By his mode of argument one could impeach the doctor's attribution of a prevailing low health in a certain district to—perhaps—a malarial atmosphere, by instancing the fact that a baby recovering from the measles had actually grown more robustious than ever.

Another has ciphered out the cause of the fall of silver to the fact that at the height of productivity of the Comstock lode it cost only 15 *cts.* to raise an *oz.* of it. As I understand it, there was lifted with every dollars' worth of silver about a dollars' worth of gold, then that ought to have lowered gold, too, ought it not? I wonder how much it cost to raise that thousand-dollar gold nugget found at Downeysville?

I must not forget Wall Street's ubiquitious and ever-present Widow. Her Bank Deposit—not much— but her little all, the result of her self-denying thrift and industry,–it would be cruel to cheapen her dollars. Well, the bimetallic heart is not unmindful of her case, and takes the liberty of whispering this in her ear: Your banker is no doubt entirely trustworthy. His advice to you any time these last fifteen years, that your little estate was better in money drawing a low 4% than in any other form practicable for you, is as wise and prudent as it is unquestionably sincere. It is very true that the policy we urge will cheapen your dollars. They will not go so far in the real estate, dry goods or grocery market, *i. e.* all prices will rise. We admit that. We affirm that. We champion it and parade it as a universal beneficence. Your dollars are now "appreciated," are worth more by, say 40%, than they were in 1873, and than they will be under free coinage. But how are you going to realize upon that appreciation? Is it not a delusive gain? You can never harvest that increase but by *buying*, and not by buying, except as prices rise after you have converted your money into property. So with a prospect of a bimetallic rise of prices, you have a chance to realize the "make" of that corner. But your Banker. interpreting your own feeling, may tell you with your in-experience in managing property and with the decrepi-tude of age coming on, money in bank on interest is better for you. We say amen. But in this country your money ought to yield you at least 6%, and will easily do so when rising prices stimulate business; and your increased income will go farther then than your present one does now. Besides you will have the very noble, if not entirely "businesslike" satisfaction of seeing your neighbor's acres, homestead, shop and mill rise, say 25%, in solid realized value, and every product of his toil be in brisk demand at correspondingly increased prices.˙ In reply to all of which the poor monometallic financier will shake his puzzled head and express a sage doubt about there being any improvement of prices at all, though he is very sure dollars will be much cheaper. The poor, economic imbecility! And his name is Legion!!

Another says that the volume of metallic money has little or nothing to do in regulating prices, for paper and other credit devices do about all the work. Of course that is insincerity pure and simple, for he is the same fellow who shouted himself hoarse in portraying the financial calamities sure to come when gold should begin to go abroad, as he predicted between winks that it soon would. These are fair specimens of their arguments,—fair specimens did I say? they are the most conspicuous and oft-repeated ones. They are all characterized by speciousness, insincerity and imbecility, combined in varying proportions, and I must not waste valuable time by further reference to them.

There is nothing left then for discussion but the mode of coming to it, so as to avoid scare or shock to the alarmists. Well, Mr. Warner's scheme of buying all the silver offered at market price, paying for it in certificates, till the market ratio of 16 is reached, then free coinage on private account to both metals alike will do it. This scheme has the merit of giving the treasury the benefit of the temporary difference, and it will prevent those wicked "Silver Kings" from making anything on the rise of silver.

That crowning economic blunder of the ages, by depressing prices, destroys the equities of contracts, cripples the machinery of distribution, provokes strife between capital and labor and wasteful and blind methods of redress, discourages enterprise, lessens profits of capital, enforces idleness and privation in the midst of plenty, and is hostile to all wealth-producing activity.

I am not painting a picture. I am expounding a law and pointing a tendency. I am no croaker. I believe this the best age industrially the world ever saw. The very poorest have a vastly better chance of life than the corresponding classes had 100 or even 50 years ago. It is not true that the rich are growing richer and the poor poorer, only in the same sense as the difference between the educated and the uneducated is also growing wider. Differentiation on all conceivable lines is of the essence of Civilization. It is incident to all progress that the forward movement should be at unequal rates in different parts of the moving mass. Nor do I bate one jot of heart and hope of our country's destined primacy in commerce, wealth, arts and all the conditions of greatness and social well-being. The exhaustless resources of our soil and mines, our courage and aptitude to new situations and conditions, all conspire to give us an unparalleled increase of the common wealth. It only remains to repair the wrong of 1873, and so to restore to health and equity all our industrial relations.